Fairies
COOKBOOK

Barbara Beery

Gibbs Smith, Publisher
TO ENRICH AND INSPIRE HUMANKIND

Salt Lake City | Charleston | Santa Fe | Santa Barbara

First Edition
16 15 14   19 18 17 16 15 14 13 12 11

Published by
Gibbs Smith, Publisher
P.O. Box 667
Layton, Utah 84041

Orders: 1.800.835.4993
www.gibbs-smith.com

Designed by Sheryl Dickert Smith
Printed and bound in China

Library of Congress Cataloging-in-Publication Data

Beery, Barbara, 1954-
  Fairies cookbook / Barbara Beery. — 1st ed.
     p. cm.
  ISBN-13: 978-1-4236-0290-3
  ISBN-10: 1-4236-0290-0
  1. Cookery—Juvenile literature. 2. Fairies in art—Juvenile literature.
I. Title.

TX652.5.B364 2007
641.5—dc22
                              2007011839

Contents

Magic Bonbon Cookies

Ingredients List

- 1 cup butter
- 2 cups flour
- ¼ cup sugar
- ⅛ teaspoon salt
- 2 teaspoons vanilla
- Red, yellow and food coloring
- ½ cup powdered sugar

Makes 36 cookies

Let's get rolling!

Preheat oven to 300 degrees F.

In a large saucepan, melt butter. Turn off heat and add flour, sugar, salt, and vanilla. Stir until dough binds together and forms a dough ball. Remove dough from saucepan and place on work area. Be careful; it's very warm!

Divide dough into 3 equal portions and drop a few drops of a different food coloring into each portion. Knead color into each dough portion until color is swirled through.

Form dough into small 1-inch balls and place 1 inch apart on foil-lined cookie sheet. Bake for 30 minutes or until very slightly browned.

Remove from oven and cool for 10 minutes.

Put powdered sugar into a medium-sized bowl and roll each ball in powdered sugar to coat. Store cookies between layers of waxed paper.

Visions of sugarplums will dance in your head!

Fancy Fairy Cakes

Ingredients List

Fairy Cakes

½ cup butter, softened

½ cup sugar

2 large eggs

¾ cup self-rising cake flour

1 teaspoon vanilla

2–3 tablespoons milk

Assorted pastel paste or powder food coloring

Frosting

1 pound vanilla candy coating or vanilla almond bark

Assorted pastel paste food coloring

Assorted decorative candies such as jimmies, sprinkles, candied or sugared flowers, fresh fruits, or cherries

Makes 6 small cakes

Let's get baking!

Preheat oven to 400 degrees F.

Using an electric mixer, combine butter, sugar, eggs, flour, vanilla, and milk.

Generously spray six small 2 to 4-inch brioche pans or decorative baking dishes with nonstick cooking spray. Place all dishes on a sheet pan and then fill each half full with batter.

Bake 20 to 25 minutes, or until cakes are golden brown on top.

Cool for 5 minutes and remove from pan. Finish cooling cakes on a wire rack.

Melt half of the candy coating according to package directions and then divide the melted candy coating between three small bowls.

Add a different coloring to each bowl, using a very tiny amount. Dip the end of a butter knife into the food coloring and then mix the color into the candy coating with the knife. Add more if needed and stir well to blend.

Spoon the candy coating frosting evenly over the six cakes, letting the frosting run down the sides of each one. Smooth out the excess frosting on top and decorate with the assorted decorative candies.

Fancy fairy fun!

Frosted Brownies

Ingredients List

Brownies

- 1 cup butter, room temperature
- 1 cup sugar
- 2 eggs
- 2 teaspoons vanilla
- 2 cups flour
- ½ cup powdered cocoa

Frosting

- 2 cups powdered sugar
- 2 tablespoons butter, room temperature
- 2 tablespoons milk or cream
- 1 teaspoon vanilla
- Assorted food coloring
- Assorted candies and sprinkles, optional

Makes 24 brownies

Let's get baking!

Preheat oven to 350 degrees F.

In a large bowl, cream butter and sugar with a hand mixer.

Add eggs, one at a time, mixing well after each one. Add vanilla.

In a separate bowl, combine flour and cocoa and whisk until blended. Add flour mixture to butter mixture and combine until smooth and free of lumps.

Pour batter into two 8 x 8-inch pans (or one 9 x 13-inch pan) that have been lined with foil and sprayed with nonstick cooking spray. The length of the foil used should be about 2 inches longer than the pan. This allows you to pull it out easily and remove the baked brownie in one giant piece.

Bake 18 to 20 minutes for the smaller pans and 25 to 30 minutes for the larger pan.

Remove brownies from oven and allow them to cool in pan for 10 minutes; then pull out of pan and cool another 10 minutes. Cut into assorted shapes with 2 to 3-inch cookie cutters.

A happily-ever-after treat!

In a mixing bowl, combine powdered sugar, butter, milk or cream, and vanilla with a hand mixer. Divide frosting into smaller bowls. Using a couple of drops of assorted food coloring, color each frosting a different color, such as pale pink, lavender, yellow, and so on.

Frost each cutout brownie with frosting and decorate with sprinkles and candies, if desired.

Butterfly Fairy Masks

Ingredients List

¼ cup flour, plus 2 tablespoons for work area

¼ cup powdered sugar

1 roll refrigerated sugar cookie dough

Ready-made vanilla frosting

Assorted sugar sprinkles, jimmies, and colorful small candies

Makes 8 to 10 cookie masks

Let's get baking!

Preheat oven to 350 degrees F.

Line a cookie sheet with foil and spray with nonstick cooking spray.

In a large bowl, knead ¼ cup flour and powdered sugar into cookie dough. Cover and refrigerate for 10 minutes.

Dust work area with remaining 2 tablespoons of flour and roll out dough about ½ inch thick. Using a 2 to 3-inch heart-shaped cookie cutter, cut out 2 hearts per mask. Lay hearts on cookie sheet overlapping the pointed ends of each heart and press down slightly to shape the dough into one piece.

Insert small pretzels into the dough (as shown in photograph) to form the butterfly's antennae.

Using a very small cookie cutter, or with the tip of a butter knife, cut out oval-shaped circles in center of each heart for the eyes.

Bake cookies for 12 minutes.

Remove from oven and cool 10 minutes. Then frost and decorate with assorted candies.

Perfect masks for a fairy ball!

Sugar-Cone Fairy Hats

Ingredients List

8 unfrosted sugar cookies, each about 3 inches in diameter

1 can vanilla frosting, tinted with food coloring or plain

Assorted food coloring, optional

2 cups popped popcorn

1 cup assorted small candies like Skittles, M&Ms, or Neccos

8 sugar cones

Assorted sprinkles, candy decorations, or mini marshmallows

Makes 8 fairy hats

Let's get decorating!

Place sugar cookies on a cookie sheet. If tinting frosting, add coloring and mix in can until well blended. Frost one side of each cookie.

Hold the cone in one hand. Grab a small amount of popcorn and candy and fill each cone about ½ full. While holding the filled cone, carefully take the frosted side of the cookie and place it over the open end of the cone. Turn it over and set the cone on the cookie base on the cookie sheet. Repeat with the remaining cones.

Now the fun begins! Using a little frosting on each piece of candy, decorate your sugar-cone fairy hat.

Chill in the refrigerator for 10 minutes or covered for up to 2 hours until ready to use.

To serve, place on a plate. The surprise comes when you break it apart to take a bite—all the hidden goodies fall out to surprise your friends!

A magical surprise in every hat!

Sugar-and-Spice Sandwich Swirls

Ingredients List

- 2 tablespoons sugar mixed with ¼ teaspoon ground cinnamon
- 2 tablespoons softened cream cheese
- 4 slices white or whole wheat bread, crusts removed
- 2 tablespoons strawberry or raspberry jam or preserves
- Powdered sugar or sprinkles

Makes 16 sandwiches

Let's get rolling!

Add cinnamon-sugar mixture to cream cheese and mix to blend.

Carefully spread a small amount of cream cheese mixture evenly on one side of each slice of bread.

Next spread a thin layer of jam or preserves on top of the cream cheese layer.

Roll each bread slice jelly-roll style and then place seam side down on a cutting board. Cut each sandwich roll into four equal slices.

Place sandwich swirls on a fancy plate and sprinkle with a little powdered sugar "fairy dust" or sprinkles.

Sugar and spice and everything nice!

Fruity Magic Wands

Ingredients List

Assorted fruits such as melons, pineapple, apples, grapes, strawberries, and starfruit

8 (6-inch) wooden skewers

Makes 8 fruit kabobs

Let's get going!

Slice melons, pineapple, apples, and starfruit into 1-inch-thick slices. The grapes and strawberries are already bite size.

Thread fruits on wooden skewers to make kabobs.

A magic wand that you can eat!

Fairy Garden Cottages

Ingredients List

Icing

4 cups powdered sugar

3 tablespoons meringue powder

¼–½ cup warm water

½ teaspoon vanilla

Assorted food coloring, optional

Houses

6 extra-large fruit or bran muffins, paper liners removed

12 whole graham crackers, broken into sections

Assorted sprinkles, small colored candies, and marshmallows

Makes 6 fairy houses

Let's get decorating!

In a bowl using an electric mixer, beat powdered sugar, meringue powder, water, and vanilla on low speed until combined. Then beat on medium to high speed until very glossy and stiff peaks form, about 5 minutes. If necessary, to get the right consistency, add more powdered sugar or water. Divide into several small bowls and add food coloring, if using.

Place about 3 tablespoons of the icing on top of a muffin. Take each graham cracker and place a small amount of icing on each. Attach the crackers with the icing and place on top of the muffin to form a roof.

Let the frosting on the graham crackers harden for a few minutes, and then spread some icing on the top and sides of the graham cracker roof and decorate the roof and house with assorted candies.

A cottage fit for a fairy!

Flower Power Fairy Food

Ingredients List

- 2 cups popped popcorn
- 1 cup craisins
- 1 cup golden raisins
- 2 cups small pretzel sticks
- 1 cup pastel milk chocolate candies
- 1 cup pastel candy-coated almonds

Makes 8 servings

Let's get mixing!

In a large mixing bowl, gently toss all the ingredients together.

Serve in small 2 to 3-inch clean, unused flowerpots.

You'll get plenty of power from this crunchy mix!

Fairy-Tale Bird's-Nest Cookies

Ingredients List

½ pound vanilla candy coating

Powdered or paste blue food coloring

2 cups chow mein noodles

2 cups coarsely chopped cornflakes

¼ teaspoon salt

½ cup shredded coconut, tinted green with liquid food coloring*

½ cup pastel candy-coated chocolate candies or small jelly beans

Makes 10 to 12 cookies

Let's get cooking!

Melt candy coating according to package directions. Stir in a very small amount of food coloring to tint the candy coating a pale blue.

In a large bowl, combine chow mein noodles, cornflakes, and salt. Pour melted candy coating over mixture, stirring until completely coated. Form nests by mounding heaping tablespoonfuls of the mixture onto a sheet pan lined with foil. Sprinkle coconut on top and then, with your thumb, make an indention in the center of each little nest. Place several candies or jelly beans into each nest.

Refrigerate about 10 minutes until firm.

* To tint coconut, place in a small ziplock plastic bag. Add a few drops of food coloring, seal bag, and shake. Voila! Colored coconut!

A treat to make the birds sing!

Fairy Queen Quiches

Ingredients List

- 1 (17.3 ounce) package refrigerated piecrusts
- ½ cup grated Swiss cheese
- 2 eggs
- ½ teaspoon salt
- ⅛ teaspoon pepper
- 2 tablespoons cream
- 5–6 cherry tomatoes, sliced

Makes 10 to 12 individual quiches

Let's get baking!

Preheat oven to 400 degrees F.

Generously spray a mini muffin pan with non-stick cooking spray. Cut out the piecrusts with a 2 to 3-inch circle or flower-shaped cookie cutter. Place each cutout inside a muffin cup.

Place approximately 1 teaspoon grated Swiss cheese into the bottom of each pastry shell.

In a medium-sized bowl, combine eggs, salt, pepper, and cream. Pour into pastry shells, filling each almost to the top.

Sprinkle with 1 teaspoon grated Swiss cheese and bake for 10 to 12 minutes or until golden brown and slightly puffed. Remove from oven and cool 5 minutes before removing each quiche from pan. Garnish with a cherry tomato slice.

Tiny bites that will delight!

Flower Petal Punch

Ingredients List

- 2 (8 ounce) bottles drinking water
- 1 bunch mint leaves
- Assorted edible flower petals such as carnations, geraniums, marigolds, roses, or pansies
- 2 liters any fruit-flavored sparkling water, chilled
- 2 liters Gatorade (blue, green, or orange), chilled
- 1 lemon, thinly sliced

Makes 12 servings

Let's get mixing!

Fill two ice cube trays with bottled water.

Add a mint leaf or edible flower petals to each ice cube square.

Freeze at least 2 hours.

Pour chilled fruit-flavored sparkling water and Gatorade into a large glass punch bowl.

Add lemon slices and flower petal ice cubes.

Decorate with a few extra flowers or flower petals.

A delicate drink for garden fairies!

Rainbow Confetti Parfait

Ingredients List

- ½ cup sugar
- 3 tablespoons cornstarch
- ¼ teaspoon salt
- 2 cups milk
- 1 teaspoon vanilla
- 1 tablespoon butter
- Assorted food coloring
- Whipped cream and rainbow sprinkles for garnish
- Colored mini marshmallows for garnish, optional

Makes 4 to 6 parfaits

Let's get cooking!

In a bowl, combine sugar, cornstarch, and salt.

In a medium saucepan over medium heat, heat milk until bubbles form around the edges.

Pour sugar mixture into hot milk, a little at a time, stirring to dissolve. Continue to cook and stir until mixture thickens enough to coat the back of a metal spoon. Do not boil.

Remove from heat, and stir in vanilla and butter. Divide pudding into thirds and tint each portion with a different food coloring. Color one pink, one green, and one yellow or orange.

Divide evenly among 4 to 6 parfait glasses, layering each pudding color. Cover and chill at least 2 hours before serving.

Garnish with a dollop of whipped cream, rainbow sprinkles, and mini marshmallows, if desired.

You'll find yourself over the rainbow!

Unicorn Calzones

Ingredients List

- 1 can refrigerated crescent rolls
- 2 tablespoons flour for work area
- 2 tablespoons butter, softened
- 8 thin slices of deli ham or turkey
- 4 sticks string cheese, each cut into 4 pieces
- Poppy seeds, optional

Makes 8 calzones

Let's get rolling!

Preheat oven to 375 degrees F.

Unroll each crescent roll on a lightly floured work area. Turn to coat each side of roll.

Put ½ teaspoon of softened butter on each piece of dough, top with 1 slice of ham or turkey, and finish with 2 small chunks of string cheese.

Roll up dough from the widest side and form into a straight horn shape.

Place each horn 2 inches apart on a foil-lined cookie sheet sprayed with nonstick cooking spray. Sprinkle poppy seeds on top, if using.

Bake 12 to 15 minutes until golden brown and puffy. Remove from oven, cool 5 minutes, and serve. Good hot from the oven or at room temperature.

Enchantingly good!

Pastel Pretzel Rings

Ingredients List

12 frozen dough dinner rolls, thawed

2 tablespoons flour for work area

Assorted liquid food coloring

Water

Q-tips

Kosher salt, optional

Cinnamon and sugar, optional

Makes 6 pretzel rings

A fairy pretzel ring is a really cool thing!

Let's get rolling!

Preheat oven to 375 degrees F.

Lightly dust work area with flour and spray your hands with nonstick cooking spray. Take each unbaked dinner roll and turn it over in the flour to lightly coat each side. Roll dough back and forth between the palms of your hands to form each roll into a snake shape.

To make a pretzel ring, take 1 snake-shaped piece of dough and link the ends together to form a ring. Then take a second piece of dough and thread it through the ring. Hook the ends of the second piece of dough together. Now you have 2 linked rings, kind of like a paper chain. Repeat these steps until all dough is used. You will have 6 pretzel rings.

Place pretzel rings 2 inches apart on a foil-lined cookie sheet that has been sprayed with non-stick cooking spray.

Put several drops of different food coloring in several small bowls and mix each with $\frac{1}{2}$ teaspoon water. Using a Q-tip like a paintbrush, decorate each pretzel ring with assorted colors.

You may sprinkle each pretzel ring with kosher salt or a blend of cinnamon and sugar if desired.

Bake for 15 to 20 minutes until lightly browned. Remove from oven, cool 5 minutes, and serve.

Mystical Moon Pies

Ingredients List

1 (7 ounce) jar marsh-mallow crème

Assorted food coloring

24 chocolate wafer cookies, non-filled

Assorted candy decorations and sprinkles

Makes 12 cookie pies

Let's get stacking!

Put ½ cup marshmallow crème in each of three different bowls. Add a different food coloring to each bowl and stir to blend.

Take a wafer cookie and place about ½ teaspoon marshmallow crème on top. Place another matching wafer on top. The rounded side of the wafer should be placed on top of the marshmallow crème. Repeat process.

Place a dollop of marshmallow crème on top cookie. Experiment and have fun with different color combinations.

Garnish the top of each moon pie with candy decorations of your choice. Serve immediately.

A magical little cookie pie!

Sparkling Star Jelly Gems

Ingredients List

½ cup butter, softened

¾ cup sugar

1 egg

1 teaspoon vanilla

½ teaspoon almond extract

2 cups flour

½ teaspoon baking soda

½ teaspoon salt

Assorted flavors and colors of jelly or jam

Makes 36 cookies

Let's get baking!

Preheat oven to 375 degrees F.

Cream butter in a large mixing bowl. Add sugar, beating until light and fluffy. Add egg, vanilla, and almond extract and mix well.

Add flour, soda, and salt to the creamed mixture, blending well.

Divide dough in half. Refrigerate one half while working with the other half. Roll each portion to ½ inch thickness on lightly floured work area. Cut out cookies with a 2 to 3-inch star cookie cutter.

Place cookies 2 inches apart on cookie sheets that have been sprayed with nonstick cooking spray. With your index finger, press a little indention in the center of each cookie and fill the center with ½ teaspoon jelly or jam.

Bake for 8 to 10 minutes or until lightly browned. Remove to wire racks to cool.

You'll be a star with these little gems!

Fancy Pink Fairy Cocoa

Ingredients List

- ½ cup white chocolate chips
- 2 cups whole milk
- ½ teaspoon vanilla
- 2 tablespoons maraschino cherry juice
- 2 large marshmallows
- ¼ teaspoon cornstarch

Makes 2 servings

Let's get stirring!

Put white chocolate chips in a mixing bowl.

Heat the milk in a small saucepan until steaming. Do not bring to a boil.

Pour heated milk over chocolate chips. Add vanilla and maraschino cherry juice. Whisk to blend. Fill 2 cups with the cocoa mixture.

Take marshmallows and dust with cornstarch. Flatten each marshmallow with your hand by pressing down slightly.

Using a ½-inch heart-shaped pastry cutter, cut a heart shape out of each marshmallow.

Garnish cocoa with marshmallow hearts.

A sweet sipping treat!

Baked Snowflakes

Ingredients List

- 10 fajita-size flour tortillas, room temperature
- 1 tablespoon butter, melted
- Assorted colored sugars
- ½ cup powdered sugar

Makes 10 treats

Let's get baking!

Preheat the oven to 350 degrees F.

Fold each tortilla into quarters and then snip out shapes with clean kitchen scissors as if you were making a paper snowflake. If your tortillas are stiff, soften them in the microwave for 15 seconds.

Place the snowflakes on a foil-lined cookie sheet, brush lightly with melted butter, and sprinkle each with assorted colors of sugar.

Bake 5 to 7 minutes or until the edges are very lightly browned. Remove from the oven and cool 5 minutes.

Dust with powdered sugar and serve.

Only a fairy could bake a snowflake!

Pink Fairy Ice-Cream Cupcakes

Ingredients List

- 1 quart vanilla ice cream or frozen yogurt
- 2 tablespoons powdered pink lemonade mix
- 24 baked yellow cupcakes
- 24 maraschino cherries, with stems

Makes 24 cupcakes

Let's get scooping!

Remove ice cream from freezer and let soften about 20 minutes; spoon into a bowl.

Stir 2 tablespoons pink lemonade mix into the softened ice cream until well blended.

Place 2 to 3 spoonfuls of the ice cream frosting onto each cupcake and pile it high.

Place a cherry on top with the stem pointing up.

Put cupcakes on a cookie sheet or in muffin tins and then place in the freezer for at least 1 hour.

A perfect treat with a simple wave of your magic wand!

Snowy Popcorn Cupcakes

Ingredients List

1 box white cake mix

Milk

1 teaspoon vanilla

½ teaspoon almond extract

4 cups popped popcorn

1 can vanilla frosting

1 cup white chocolate chips

½ cup candy decorations

Makes 24 cupcakes

Let's get baking!

Preheat oven to 350 degrees F.

Make cake mix according to package directions, but substitute milk for water. Add vanilla and almond extracts to the batter and stir to blend.

Fill a muffin pan with paper liners and spray generously with nonstick cooking spray.

Divide batter evenly between 24 muffin cups using an ice-cream scoop to keep the amount of batter equal between cups.

Bake and cool according to package directions on cake mix.

Fill a large bowl with the popcorn.

Frost each cupcake generously with frosting and then dip each frosted cupcake into the popcorn.

Add white chocolate chips and candy decorations to fill in the spots where popcorn did not stick to the frosting.

Let it snow, let it snow, let it snow!

Fairy Princess Marshmallow Pops

Ingredients List

- Assorted candies and sprinkles
- 1 pound vanilla candy coating or vanilla almond bark
- 12 craft sticks, colored or plain
- 12 large marshmallows, colored or white

Makes 12 pops

Let's get dipping!

Place assorted candies and sprinkles in several small bowls.

Melt 6 squares of vanilla coating according to package directions.

Insert a craft stick into the bottom of each marshmallow.

Holding the stick, dip each marshmallow into the melted coating and then dip coated marshmallow into assorted candies.

Place marshmallow pops on a baking sheet and put in the freezer for 5 minutes to harden the coating quickly. Keep marshmallow pops in the freezer until ready to eat.

When ready to serve, tie a little ribbon around the stick for decoration, if desired.

A sweet frozen treat!

Frosty Fairy Mints

Ingredients List

- 1 (3-ounce) package cream cheese
- 2 ½ cups powdered sugar
- ½ teaspoon mint extract
- Assorted pastel food coloring
- ½ cup sugar

Makes 48 mints

Let's get mixing!

In a mixing bowl, mix cream cheese and powdered sugar together with an electric mixer.

Add mint extract to dough. Using your hands, knead dough until it begins to form a ball and is the consistency of pie dough. If the dough is too dry, add ¼ teaspoon water and blend into mixture.

Divide dough into 3 equal pieces and put 2 to 3 drops of different food coloring onto each section. Blend colors into each portion. You can leave the colors swirled in the dough, or you can completely blend the color evenly into each dough section.

Pinch off about a 2-inch piece of dough and form a ball by rolling it between the palms of your hands. Roll the ball in sugar. Flatten out dough and cut out into assorted shapes with a small 1-inch cookie cutter.

Or you can divide the dough into 1-inch pieces and roll between the palms of your hands to form small balls. Roll the balls in sugar. Then gently flatten them out with your hands.

Frosty mint treats!

Snow Queen Punch

Ingredients List

Punch

1 (2 liter) bottle lemon
lime soda

1 lemon, juiced

1 lime, juiced

2–3 drops blue food
coloring

Sugar or honey,
to taste

2 cups frozen
blueberries, optional

Garnish

½ cup blue decorating
sugar

Sliced starfruit,
optional

Makes 10 to 12
servings

Let's get stirring!

For the punch, combine all the ingredients
except frozen blueberries and stir to blend.

Sample a taste to see if it needs to be sweeter
and then sweeten according to taste with sugar
or honey.

Stir in frozen blueberries and serve.

To garnish punch cups, rub the edge of the
punch cups with the leftover lemon and lime
wedges to dampen the drinking edge of the
cup. Dip into decorating sugar. Put a slice of
starfruit on the rim of the cup, if desired.

A drink fit for a queen!

Fairy Godmother Pumpkin Puffs

Ingredients List

- 3 cups flour
- 1 cup brown sugar
- 2 tablespoons white sugar
- 4 teaspoons baking powder
- 1 teaspoon salt
- 1 teaspoon cinnamon
- 1 teaspoon nutmeg
- 1 teaspoon pumpkin pie spice
- 1 cup milk
- 1 cup canned pumpkin
- ½ cup unsweetened applesauce
- 2 eggs
- 1 teaspoon vanilla
- ¾ cup raisins, craisins, or dried blueberries, optional
- ¼ cup powdered sugar mixed with ½ teaspoon ground cinnamon

Makes 24 mini muffins

Let's get baking!

Preheat oven to 325 degrees F.

In a large bowl, mix together all ingredients except dried fruits and powdered sugar mixture with a wooden spoon and then finish mixing with an electric mixer.

If desired, stir in raisins, craisins, or dried blueberries.

Line each muffin cup with paper muffin cup liners and then spray each one lightly with nonstick cooking spray.

Fill muffin cups almost to the top and then bake 12 to 15 minutes.

Remove from oven and cool 5 minutes before removing from pan. Dust with powdered sugar mixture and serve.

Share these with your Fairy Godmother!

Tooth Fairy Treats

Ingredients List

Fruit cups

> Fruit of choice such as apples, oranges, or melons

Toppings

> Fruit of choice such as blueberries, strawberries, blackberries, melon balls, craisins, or raisins

> Vanilla frozen yogurt or fresh fruit sorbet

> Honey

Makes 4 servings

Let's get scooping!

Slice the fruit for the fruit cup in half. Cut a small slice off the bottom of each fruit half to allow it to sit flat on the serving plate.

Using a small melon baller or teaspoon, scoop out some of the fruit inside to allow for the filling and topping. Save the scooped-out fruit to use later.

Put the filling of frozen yogurt or sorbet in each fruit bowl. The amount used depends on the size of the fruit cup.

Top with assorted fruit toppings, drizzle with honey, and serve.

The Tooth Fairy will love this "tooth-friendly" treat!

Little Mermaid Shells

Ingredients List

- 1 cup sugar
- 2 eggs, room temperature
- ¾ cup butter, melted
- 1 cup flour
- ⅛ teaspoon ground nutmeg
- ½ teaspoon ground cinnamon
- ½ teaspoon vanilla
- Melted chocolate or white chocolate
- Sprinkles or jimmies
- Powdered sugar

Makes 24 little cakes

Let's get baking!

Preheat oven 350 degrees F.

Combine sugar and eggs with a whisk and whip in as much air as possible to make the batter light and fluffy. Stir in melted butter.

Add the flour, nutmeg, cinnamon, and vanilla. Mix well to combine the wet and dry ingredients.

Spray Madeleine molds (molds shaped like clam shells) generously with nonstick cooking spray and then fill each mold with about a tablespoon of batter. After the molds have been filled, tap the pan lightly on the countertop to even out the batter in each mold.

Bake until lightly browned, about 15 minutes. Cool for 1 minute and then remove from pans and cool on rack.

Dip in melted chocolate or white chocolate and decorate with sprinkles or jimmies. Or dust with powdered sugar.

A sprinkling of fun in every bite!

Pixie Pancakes

Ingredients List

- 2 cups flour
- 1 tablespoon baking powder
- ½ teaspoon salt
- 2 tablespoons sugar
- ½ teaspoon ground cinnamon
- 2 eggs
- 2 cups milk
- 3 tablespoons butter, melted
- 2 teaspoons vanilla
- 1 cup berries or sliced fruit, such as blueberries, raspberries, strawberries, kiwifruit, apples, peaches, or bananas
- Maple syrup
- ½ cup powdered sugar

Makes 20 small pancakes

Let's get mixing!

Sift the flour, baking powder, salt, sugar, and cinnamon into a large bowl.

Whisk the eggs and milk in a separate bowl, then whisk in the melted butter and vanilla. Pour the egg mixture over the dry ingredients and stir with a spoon, but do not beat. The batter will be a little bit lumpy.

Fill a ziplock bag half full of batter and seal. Cut the tip off one corner and squirt a design on a hot griddle that has been sprayed with nonstick cooking spray. Place a few pieces of fruit on the top side of the pancake, if desired. When bubbles form, flip pancake and cook 1 to 2 minutes or until done.

Remove pancakes from griddle one at a time with a spatula. Place pancakes on a plate and cover with foil. Keep in an oven at 200 degrees F until ready to serve.

When ready to serve, carefully remove pancakes from oven. Serve with warm maple syrup, additional fresh fruit, and a sprinkling of "pixie dust" powdered sugar.

Perfect pixie treats!

Woodland Fairy Mushrooms

Ingredients List

Cupcakes

- 1 package chocolate cake mix
- Milk
- 2 teaspoons vanilla

Frosting

- ½ cup butter, softened
- 4 cups powdered sugar
- ¼ teaspoon salt
- ⅓ cup whole milk or half-and-half
- 2 teaspoons vanilla
- Red paste food coloring
- White candies or white chocolate chips or nibs

Makes 20 cupcakes

Let's get baking!

Make cake mix according to package directions, but substitute milk for water and add 2 teaspoons vanilla.

Place 20 cupcake liners into cupcake pans. Divide batter into liners, filling almost full so that the tops are really big and slightly hang over the side when baked.

Bake according to package directions.

Cool cupcakes 10 minutes and then remove liners.

To make frosting, combine the butter, powdered sugar, salt, milk or half-and-half, vanilla, and food coloring until smooth. Frost cupcakes.

Decorate each cupcake with white candies for mushroom spots.

"Mushrooms" you'll love to eat!

Friendship Fairy Bread

Ingredients List

Bread

- 1 package refrigerated buttermilk biscuits (8 biscuits)
- 4 tablespoons sugar
- 4 tablespoons brown sugar
- 1 teaspoon cinnamon
- 4 tablespoons butter, melted

Icing

- ½ cup powdered sugar
- Tiny pinch of salt
- ¼ teaspoon vanilla
- 1 teaspoon milk
- Assorted food coloring
- Candy sprinkles, optional

Makes 8 little biscuits

Let's get baking!

Preheat oven to 350 degrees F.

Cut each biscuit into four equal pieces.

Mix together sugars and cinnamon in a large ziplock bag and then drop 5 to 7 biscuit pieces into the mixture, seal the bag shut, and shake. Repeat until all the pieces are coated.

Spray 8 silicone or paper muffin cup liners with nonstick cooking spray and place on a cookie sheet. Drop 4 to 6 coated biscuit pieces into each cup. Sprinkle with any remaining sugar mixture and then drizzle with melted butter.

Carefully place in the oven, and bake 10 to 12 minutes.

Remove from oven; cool slightly for a few minutes. Set aside.

Combine all the remaining ingredients and stir to blend. The icing should be runny. Take a spoonful and drizzle over each piece of Fairy Friendship Bread. Decorate with candy sprinkles if desired.

Share your friendship bread with a friend!

About the Author

Barbara Beery is the founder of Batter Up Kids Culinary Center in Austin, Texas. This national retail cooking center franchise offers culinary classes and camps, and hosts cooking birthday parties for children ages 2 through teens. For more information, check out the website at www.batterupkids.com.

Barbara is also the author of *Delicious Desserts, Sensational Snacks,* and the best-selling *Pink Princess Cookbook.*

www.gibbs-smith.com
www.batterupkids.com